Copyright © 2022 Prof Claudia Gray & Sarita Kruger

All rights reserved. This book or any portion thereof may not be reproduced or used in any manner whatsoever without the express written permission of the publisher except for the use of brief quotations in a book review.

First printed 2022

ISBN 978-1-77629-112-0

Danny chomps on TOO MANY CHOCOLATES

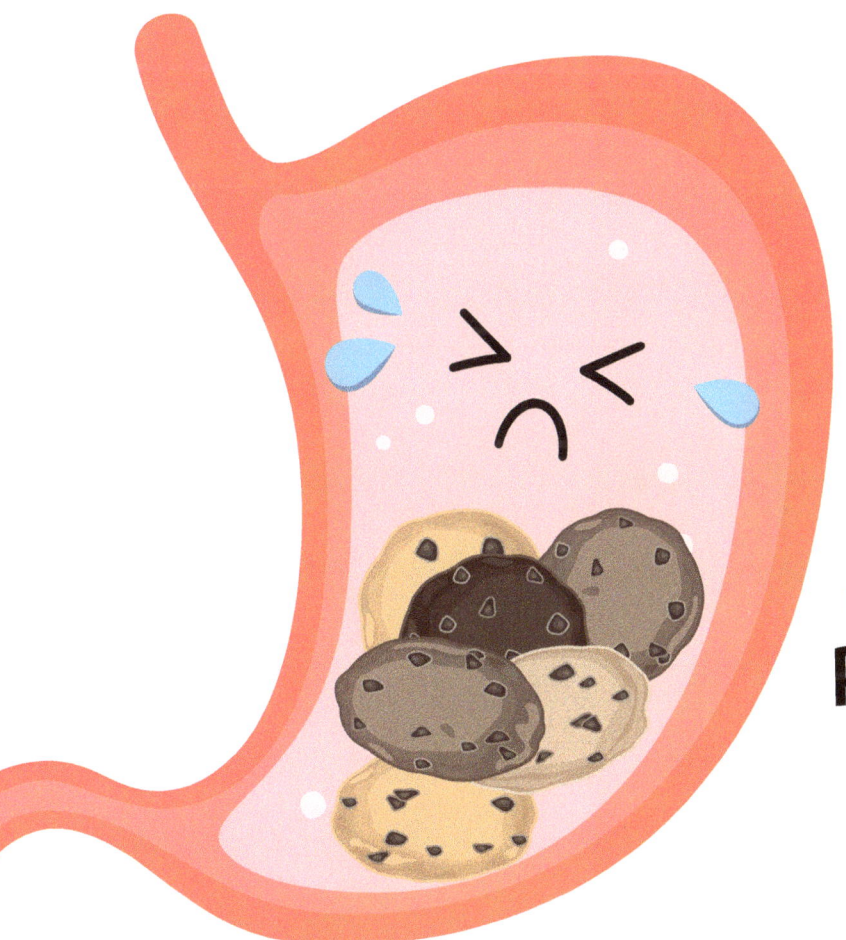

Written by Paediatrician
Prof Claudia Gray

Illustrated by
Sarita Kruger

He'd learned about balancing screen time and play.

Each evening at five when mum went for her jog, Dan would wave her goodbye and then tickle his dog,

Before settling, exhausted, upon the blue couch

For his favourite TV show: "Gary the Grouch."

And he ran to the pantry to Mum's box of treats.

The treats were delicious, he ate more and more,

Until his poor belly felt grumbly and sore,

At supper time Danny refused all his food

So he ran to the pantry for one last sweet bite,

"Aha," said his mum,
"this tells me so much
Why your lovely good dinners
have been left untouched

Our bodies need energy to keep on the go,

Just like torches need batteries to glimmer and glow.

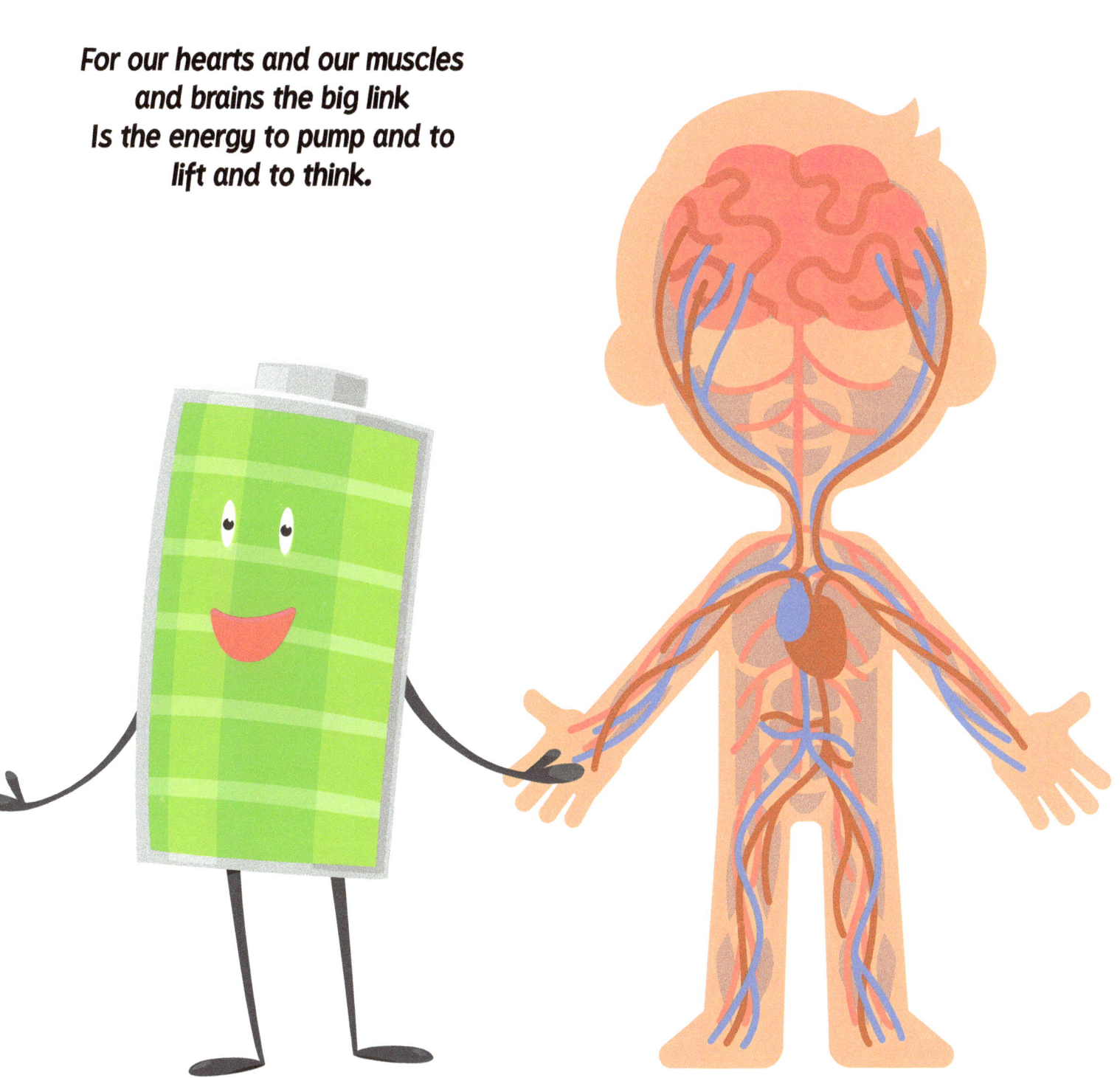

For our hearts and our muscles and brains the big link
Is the energy to pump and to lift and to think.

**Now humans, as you know, are battery-free:
So we use food and drink to get our energy!**

Just as torches need batteries of certain sizes,
We need certain foods which the body recognizes

And prevent mood and sleep time from going all wrong.

Each day we need starches called "carbohydrates" too—
That's bread, rice, and pasta; potatoes in stew.

The carbs give us energy; keep our brains beeping

We also need protein- that's
meat, chicken, fish;
Beans, lentils and eggs too
make a protein dish.

We need healthy fats too - avo, nuts, healthy oil;

And dairy, for calcium,
So bones 'n teeth don't spoil.

And fruit and veg a-plenty!
It's best five a day

For mighty strong vitamins to keep sickness away.

"Oh yes, now I see why for dinner each night
There's a meat and a starch and a vegetable bite.

And you ask me to eat cheese
and yoghurt each day
And a fruit and nut snack
before going to play!

But what about biscuits and sweets- they're so yummy... Are they any good to my body and tummy?"

The treats cause our blood sugar level to soar,
Then it crashes thereafter so we just crave more.

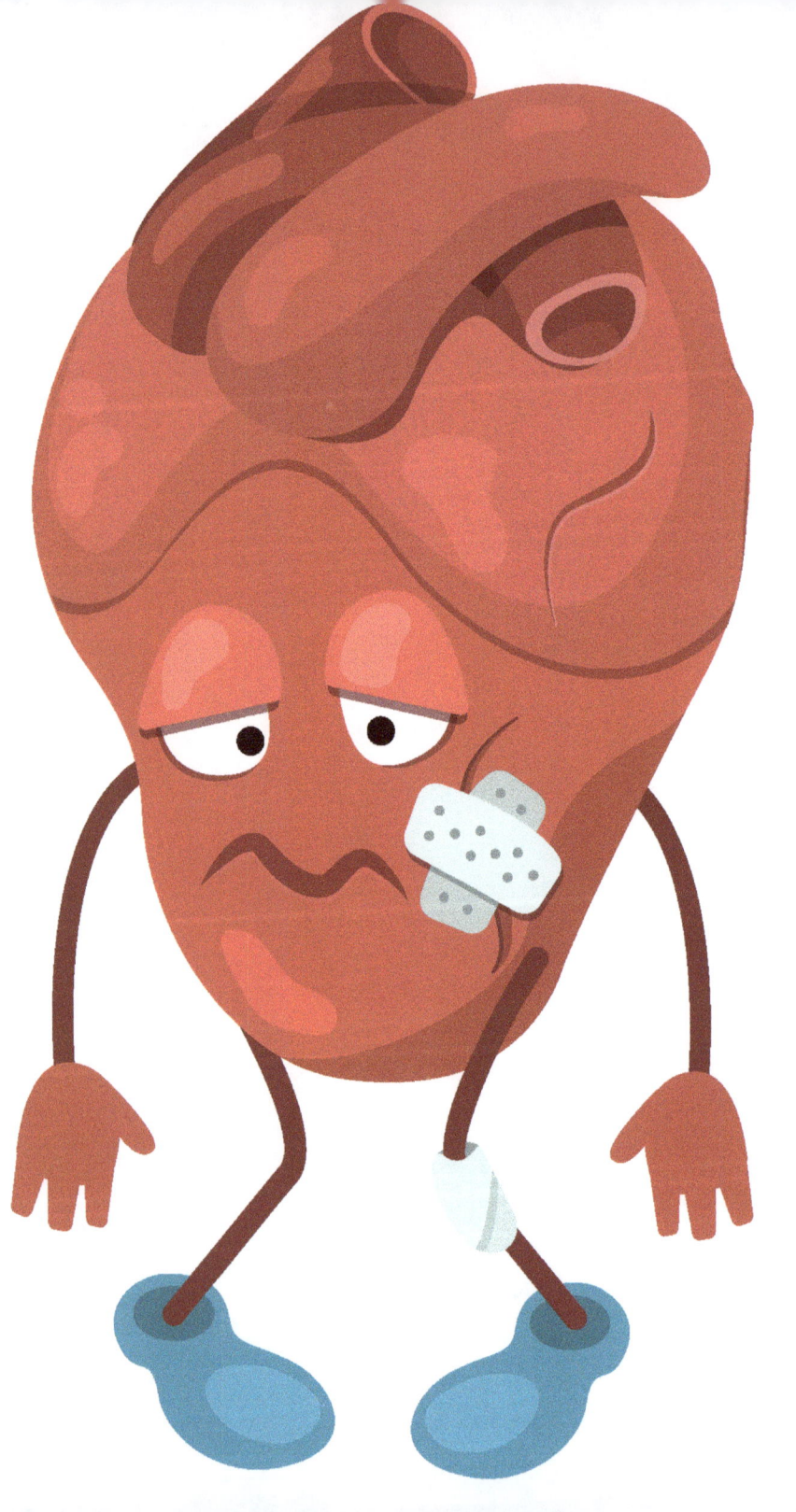

Yes nice as they are, loads of treats are not smart
And long term they put strain on your blood and your heart."

And don't confuse hunger when there's actually thirst.
Try this: when you're crazily craving a sweet,
First have apple and water, then a smaller treat.

Yes! Your best bet for excellent health education
Is to eat every food group in good "moderation!"

LET'S REVISE SOME KEY CONCEPTS IN THE BOOK:

Have a look at the "food pyramid" which shows the importance of certain foods. The foods in the bottom 4 layers of the pyramid are very very important for our health.
You've learned about carbohydrates, fruits and veg, proteins, dairy and healthy fats...do you eat these each day?

Treats are an "extra" on the top of the pyramid...they are so delicious but our body does not actually need them. A few treats are fine- especially after we've eaten our healthy meals- but too many treats cause trouble!

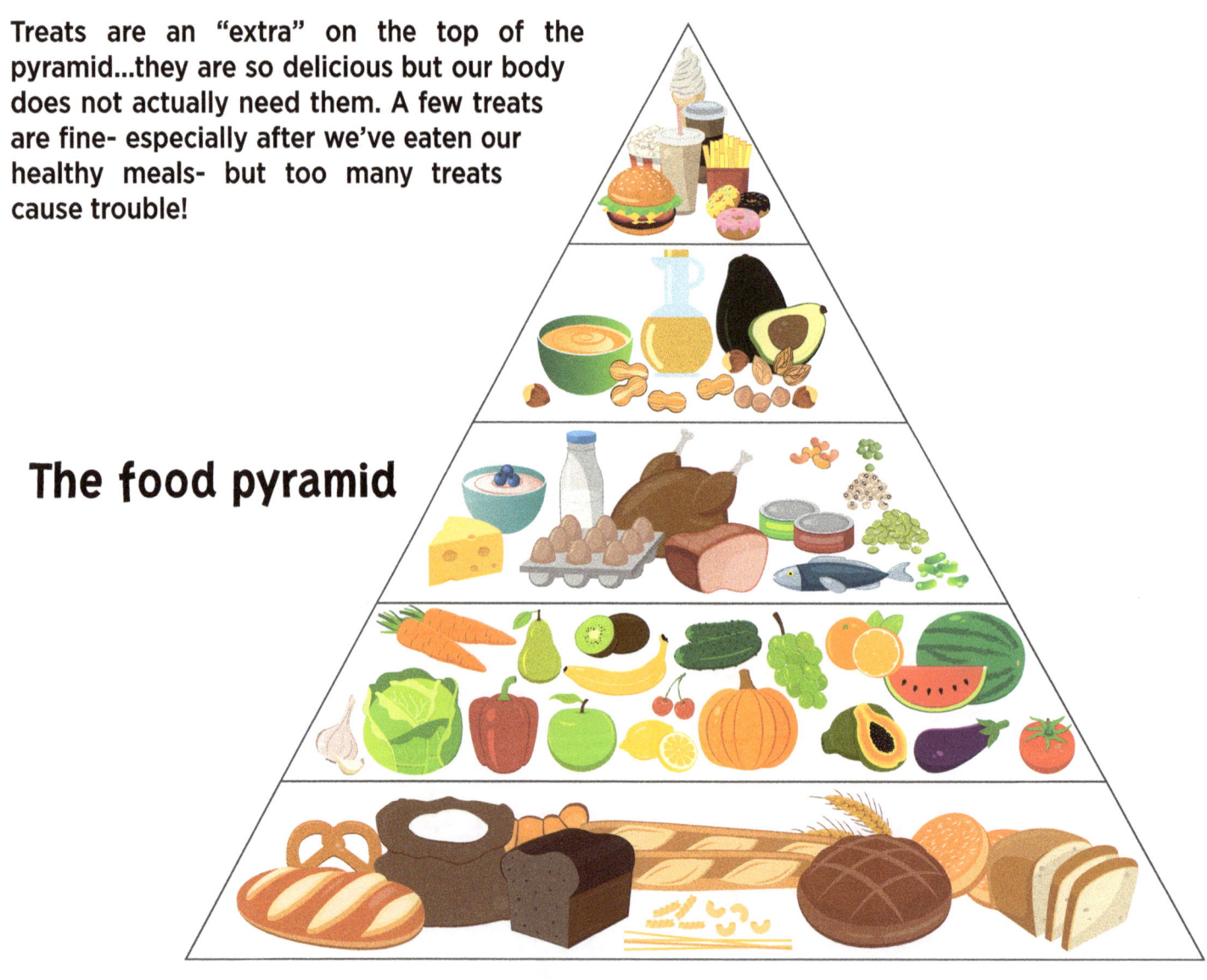

The food pyramid

Other tips for a healthy lifestyle:

EXERCISE DAILY

DRINK PLENTY OF WATER

Get a bit of sunlight each day to get our vitamin D levels up!

VITAMIN D

Some people have trouble with eating - they may have allergies so their bodies react badly to certain foods.

They may be "picky" eaters (which means they don't eat many different varieties or tastes or textures of foods).

Some people eat too many of the unhealthy foods.

We can be helped to eat a good and varied diet by a DIETITIAN, who is a person who has studied all about nutrition and food.

Other tips for a healthy lifestyle:

EXERCISE DAILY

DRINK PLENTY OF WATER

Get a bit of sunlight each day to get our vitamin D levels up!

VITAMIN D

Some people have trouble with eating - they may have allergies so their bodies react badly to certain foods.

They may be "picky" eaters (which means they don't eat many different varieties or tastes or textures of foods).

Some people eat too many of the unhealthy foods.

We can be helped to eat a good and varied diet by a DIETITIAN, who is a person who has studied all about nutrition and food.

As a young child, Claudia used to write stories for her little cousins and dreamed of becoming a "professional babysitter." Her love for children converted itself into a career as a Paediatrician, trained both in the UK and in South Africa. Claudia's life is full-to-the-brim with a busy career and 4 cherished children, which sidelined her writing career for many years. Finally, she has now had the opportunity, together with the talented Sarita as illustrator, to write a series of childrens' stories which aim to take scary situations and explain them in a fun and reassuring way.

Sarita is also a mom of 2 with a passion for design and communication. She is excited about this opportunity to visually relay Claudia's messages and reduce stress for little people.

"Our children are our greatest treasure. They are our future.
The true character of a society is revealed in how it treats its children."
Nelson Mandela